MW01143281

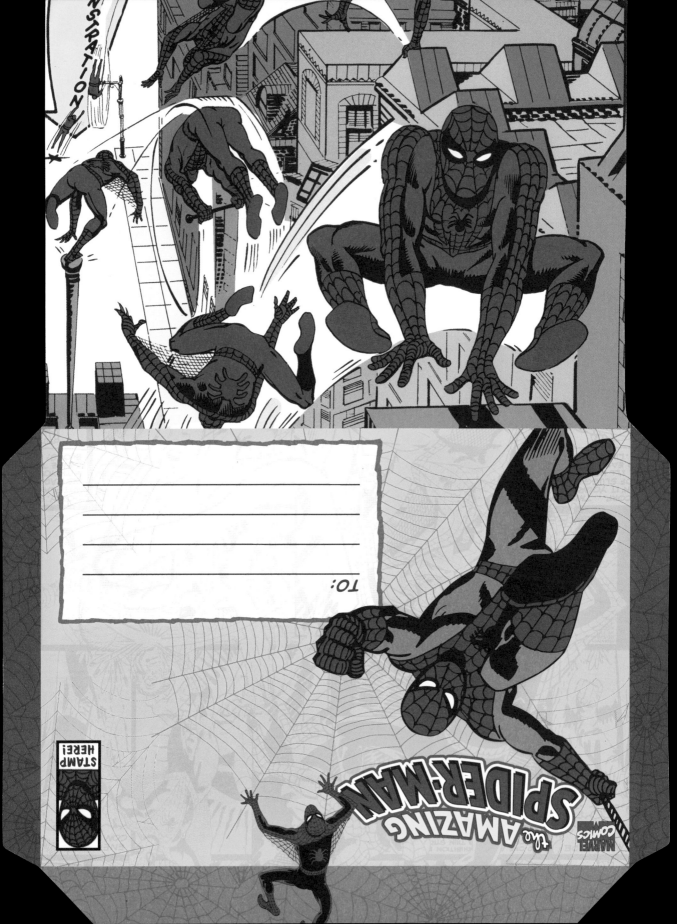

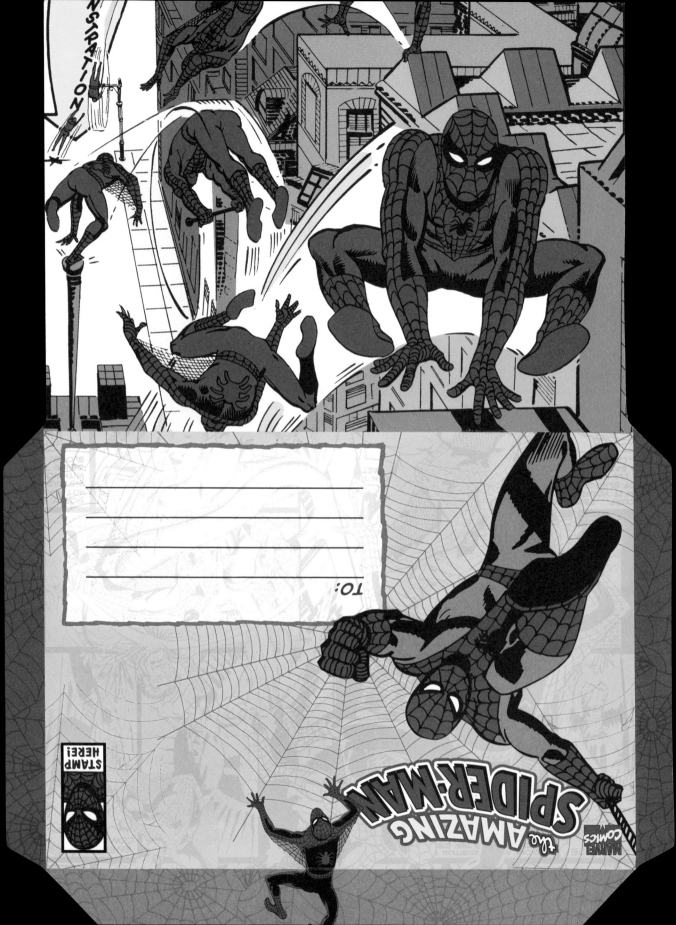

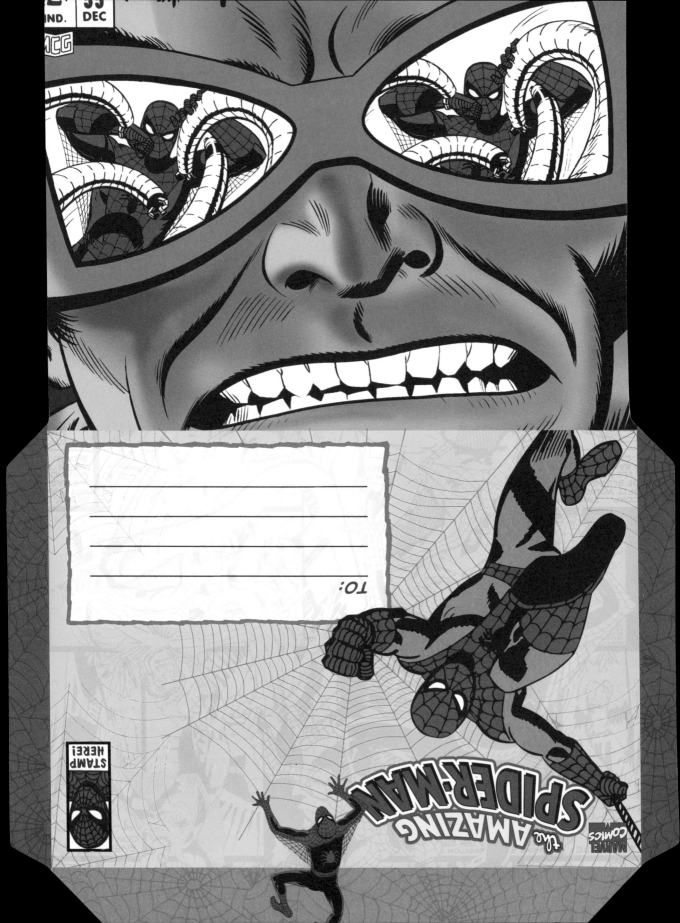

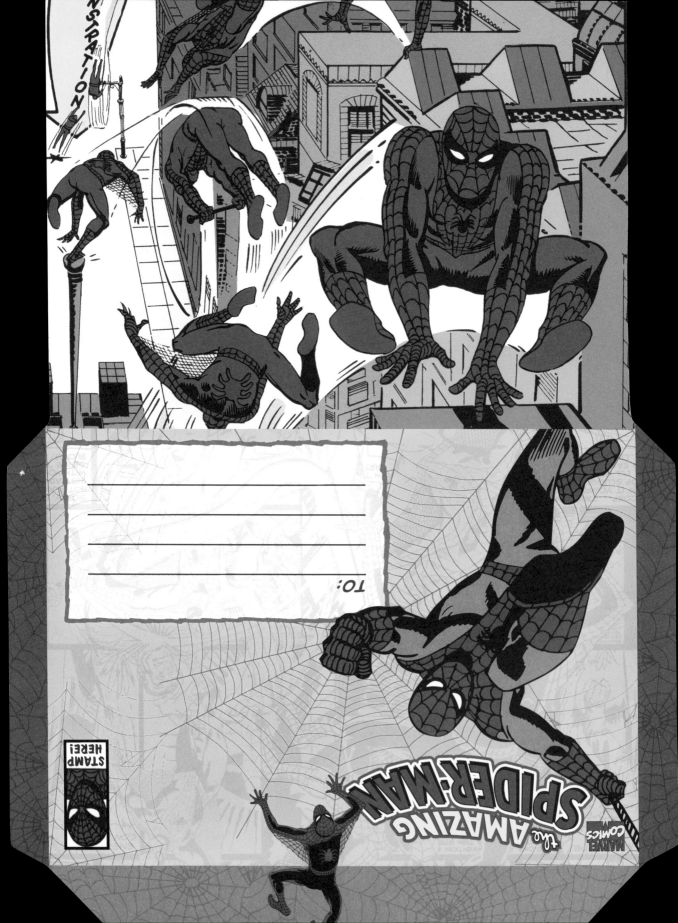

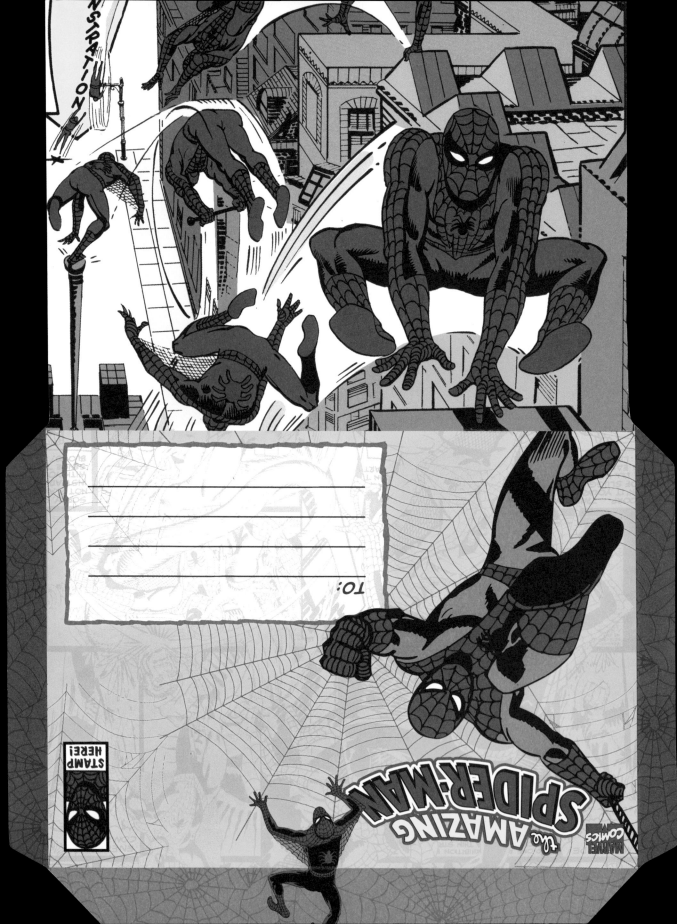

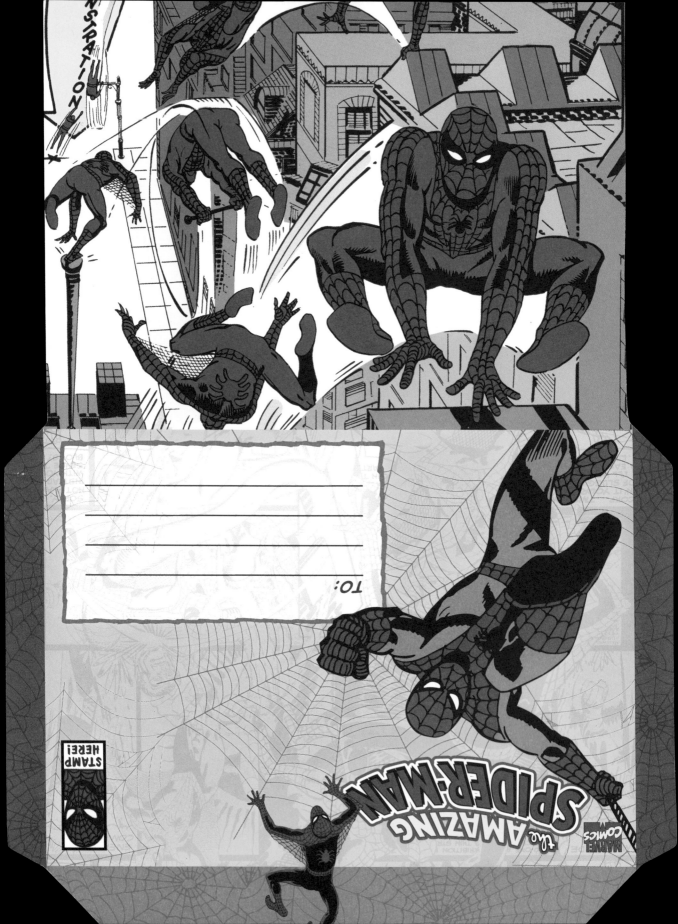

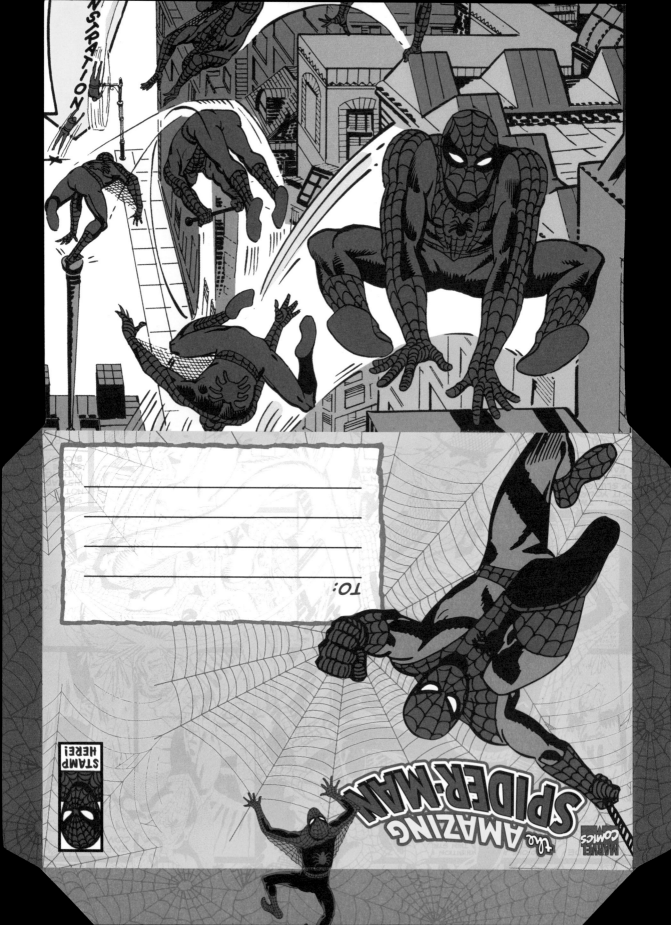

HOW CAN SPIDER-MAN DEFEAT A FOE WHO CANNOT BE INJURED?? DON'T DARE MISS.....

"NOTHING CAN STOP... THE SANDMAN!"

TO:

STAMP HERE!

the AMAZING SPIDER-MAN

MARVEL COMICS

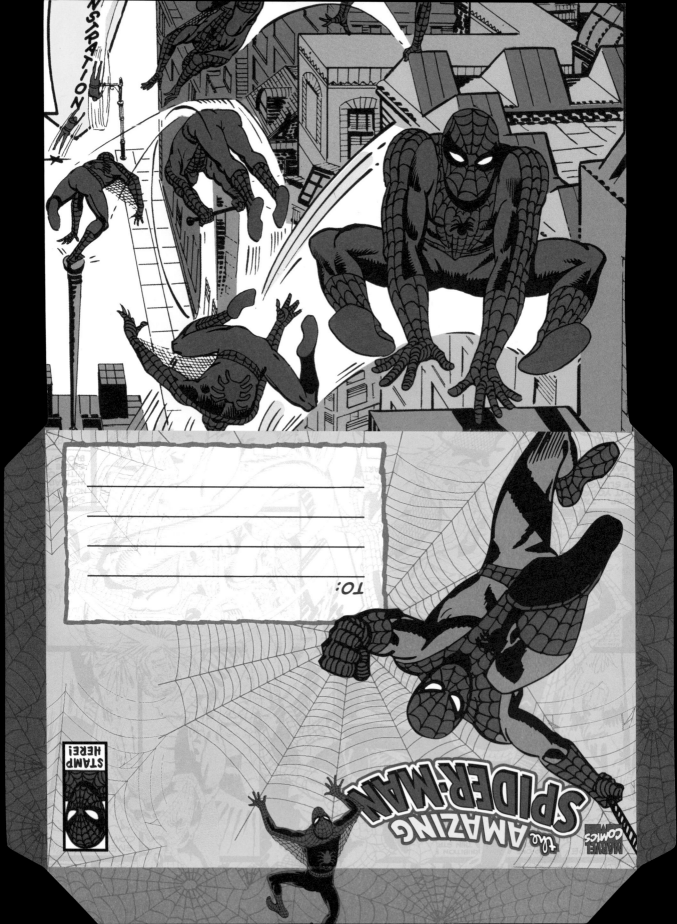

HOW CAN SPIDER-MAN DEFEAT A FOE WHO CANNOT BE INJURED?? DON'T DARE MISS......

"NOTHING CAN STOP... THE SANDMAN!"